PEOPLE YOU MAY KNOW

MICHAEL ROBINS

D0878408

Distributed by Independent Publishers Group
Chicago

Saturnalia Books
105 Woodside Rd.
Ardmore, PA 19003
info@saturnaliabooks.com

ISBN: 978-1-947817-22-7 (print), 978-1-947817-23-4 (ebook)
Library of Congress Control Number: 2020941838

Cover art and book design by Robin Vuchnich

Distributed by:
Independent Publishing Group
814 N. Franklin St.
Chicago, IL 60610
800-888-4741

Thank you to the editors of the following journals where versions of these poems first appeared: *Arsenic Lobster, Bateau, Bear Review, Columbia Poetry Review, Crazyhorse, descant, DIAGRAM, Diode Poetry Journal, Fence, Forklift, Ohio, Ghost Proposal, HYPERALLERGIC, The Laurel Review, Mississippi Review, Pine Hills Review, Pinwheel, Powder Keg Magazine,* and *TYPO.*

Thank you to those who responded to social media and other queries with title suggestions for the individual poems in this collection. Thanks especially to Joel Allegretti, Dan Chelotti, Adam Clay, Connie Clay (unbeknownst to her), Eric Dickerson, Deilani Ferguson, Corey Galloway, Sara Goodman, Richie Hofmann, J. Johnson, Ashton Legier, Ada Limón, Michael McNally-Costello, Joe Pan, Peter Richards, Ellen Simonis, Bradley Harrison Smith, Erin Elizabeth Smith, and Susan Yount.

"A Recurring Wave of Arrival" draws its title from "Self-Portrait in a Convex Mirror" by John Ashbery; "Flowers of the Field" is adopted from the opening lyric of "Flowers" on the album *Coming Home* by Leon Bridges; "Forever Is Composed of Nows" is borrowed from the opening line of "624" by Emily Dickinson; the phrase "coffee, nicotine, and paper" ("Study of Coffee, Nicotine, & Paper") is attributed to James Foley as recollected by Clare Morgana Gillis (*VICE News*); the phrase "The Odd Ring of Reality" appears in an *Atlantic Monthly* "Dispatch" written by Sandra Tsing Loh; "Meeting the Middle Western Day" is a variation on "meet the middle western day" from Lew Welch's "Chicago Poem"; "If You Meet Some Stranger" is borrowed from *Leaves of Grass* by Walt Whitman; the title "As I Bow & Pass Smiling" originates from the concluding line of "The Young Housewife" by William Carlos Williams; the phrase "These Things Astonish Me" appears in the final lines of William Carlos Williams' "Pastoral."

The poem "People You May Know" was written during a daily postcard exchange (February 2016) with Dan Chelotti. The start of every sixth line corresponds with each line in Marianne Moore's "Poetry." Phrases appearing in quotations are borrowed from "South End" and "Awkward Silence," both by James Tate.

Contents

Escape into the Day

I'd like to begin with an easing, how just now
I stood outside in Kansas, & the earth's failure
to lickety-split into the sun leaves the long,

Midwest line of morning somewhere I'd like
to crawl to, quit the slack chin & wrinkles
around my mouth, indecisive hair, & posture,

& handles. They'd discover my green shoes
where I'd waited for the spun path of the planet
I know so little about & was taken. I'd like

to abandon each darkness, for the distances
between me & that tree line to burst with crocus,
field mice, & the hawk lazy enough overhead

or just plain gratified from its last blessing
not to slice the air, & the atoms among us hims,
hers & thems to melt into a figure delicious,

awkward creatures of our elbows & knees
knocking our certain deaths a bit. Maybe,
like a bridal veil, when an elegy uncovers love

then my own impulse will defy the gravities
tugging loss. I'm beyond last night's wine,
& in a wiring that wakes before dawn I'm tired,

good god, the sputtering of little irrelevance
before, as they say, the new day & so many
satisfy the road already with its peculiar music

not like birdsong but a singing nonetheless
toward the middle of our lives, my own
circles under the eye & a straight fact anyway

I'm getting emotional. I'd like to contain
enough candor to let myself cry, bracing now
for the pendulum as the light in the corner

inches up to revive my head where I hunch
pure to this writing. Maybe we won't
disappear completely today, the molecules

surround us despite our common blindness,
believe in their sole purpose of mingling
& making love. Breakfast, & before imagining

its branch, I hold a banana's bruised crescent,
imperfect smile, hell this yellow telephone
beginning to whisper. Maybe you too

will let deliver each filament of your head,
relieve the fret of your shoulders, untie
both shoes & permit the remaining hours

to open the radiant flower on your tongue,
complete its promise & trust by our full
fleeting bodies that the world bends for light.

NATIONAL HISTORIC BATTLEFIELDS

—for Jim Tate

The fumes from all kinds of valley & scrub, these
timeworn chirps off the block to the parade ground
bygone, marched. Wilted pond, frogs, peccadillos
that, when I sink stone, dim. Leisure not exactly,
was a damn bayonet, my ditty of birdbrain hatchet
leveling hickory, the hard & soft pine, the moon I say
passing evenings with the mind lodged as in a glass
wet & cold & slid forward. Windows like musings
fall routinely dark, the schoolhouse closed & forever
another olive please, martinis particular, tomfoolery
dropping my scarf in the middle of the night, retrieving
one afternoon when my friend pegged the truth to say,
Well, it gets easier. I couldn't mend the life of me,
my marriage salient, ill-strung before it played &
plainly, this bushel of people I cherished now done,
teachers dead, pupils mulling days & soon undressing
leaves to the ground where the squirrels dig & bury
& forget. Without, I'm fine to sit long & think, to think
of sitting & long, conjure the stoplight, the cemetery
turning & the bare house on the left. Someone meets
its garden need, repairs the feeder, lightens a drink
before the ice melts clear. Well, I miss my friend
steady again at the fence, the town line to tree line
willowy & yet imagined. I make believe toy soldiers,

lead uniforms, carefully painted rifles. I'll know him
among that crowd, pinky swear, should our lamps
cross the same air. He shadows for now the ants,
the mosquitoes, the mice that move the vast woods.

Hypothetical Deathmatch

More than before I trust the unspecified
you. Lunch, gathering its things,
left us zigzagging both in the lakebed.
I believed the vincible rock, believe
me happy as any particular burst
crossing the flag while boys act cruel
like snakes with snakes. It's their nature

& she says, Let the bricks rise as down,
down go the trains. The way the earth is
only means we've made it man, irreparable.
I ride those ideas to a party & mesh
with teeth-showing laughter. It might be
ice that lifts me up, maybe in my cup
what rounds it off. The sky is &

is bewildered & in lieu of stowing a clock,
I hang notes to name the slowness
settled in the gears. At midnight you
blow the balloon, let go of the purple air
& your bangs lift. I want to forgive my ideas
copied like a bulb. By their light I wake
& know something terrible has happened.

SOMETHING LIKE PNEUMONIA

Nobody remembers the particular bird
caught one half minute Sunday by its reflection,
least of all the bird who may for that matter
be dead, danced into the hushed science
& its silence not unlike the husband & wife
tossing in separate dreams, out from under layers
frozen with sparrows before they lift in unison
their wings. In the history of a dying hour
not much happens & I pour three cups of seed,
filling the perch. I'll defer to the faraway
fields, clear my throat for the greener grass
& the glimpse of the cottontail pegged, floating
high until it's another way life says goodbye.
If I had their heads I'd talk like the flowers
&, if they'd mine, subject to terms & conditions
any breath revises, stalls in a singular room
between the slap & its belated whimper,
earnestly its blood. I'm stepping both toward
& from the busted chin & for a final spell
repeating this memory: when indeed in Amherst
marriage broke my favorite glass, I no longer
believed the patience of my neighbors, the fires
rising large those last weeks alone & burning
what wouldn't sell, what wouldn't fit with what I

couldn't spare in the trunk. I've my breath
once more, was never gone in fact & in trying
again & again to back the car in, vow to leave
inside that year certain squirrels & foxes
fare-thee-well. Of gravity working everyone
I swore this morning over my own & yet support
streamers on birthdays home, from the doctor
lollipops orange & blue unless a diagnosis
stares steadfast & hard. I'm hurrying like anyone
crossing my life ahead of the changing light,
before it fades. Some moons are yellow & some
mostly sky under which objects spiral blind,
stretch thin, faux handbags & the like.
In a dying hour I wonder what if anything
scaffolds teach us, scars barely seen & finches,
excuse me, these hunches I call my voice
drumming a bucket among coyotes in the urban
backdrop. No matter how you slice the day
she's enough a good time, carries us forward
until every car, sure, I imagine they stop.
With practice, I'll reap that labor of thought,
join the actual feathers, without substance
between the heavy lilacs & the tugging breeze.

SIDEWARD & LEISURELY CRUMBLES THE HEART'S PRESIDIO

To what do I owe the pleasure to be awakened,
croaking the AM hubbub of sunlight, trees
& their medley every which way. I trust
I startled spiders or rats or there but a tower,
not its tank, so I concluded some smolder
before bed. High in my daughter's room
I see now shadows of our house, cascading days
enthralled in being ceramic at windows
or tempting the spyglass. Inside most anything,
it's matter like perspective, reminds me of

more perfect ways to receive the fox, spotted
with my right as my left hand steals the one
who loves: he wears fabulous clothing, he's often
impressioned & say, those aren't violets in the yard.
...Those are grommets, are charlatans slipping
ice into lemonade & the porcelain polished
like a charm or where my doctor's many needles
construct a someone who wasn't. There,
did you go out likewise or count the tiled night
here, taking that better aim on the voice

owned by a friend? This one belongs to you, holds
muscle & grace while the rest are awkward bone.
Once upon a time, uh-huh, & in the end I
knew you as my brother, that the heart sails
& some find barreled whiskey & the priesthood
no different whatsoever. Actually, we
shudder now in different costumes, banks
swell on every corner & my voice belongs not
to a rich person. Behind the bottles they put candles
& make them… Alright, let's have another.

I'm not going to sing because I could. I'm not
singing because I cannot describe beauty
as sex or blokes in the backseat of a cab. There's no
expert among them but fashion is as fashion
does, walking the rumpus with sightlines
down. Even the owls seem like rhetoric bleached
& flossed, real songs saying how little we care,
what a young person's world, like, early-twenties
this is. From my daughter's room I see shadow,
see house, see you later. I've gone some other way.

FLOWERS OF THE FIELD

—for Adam & Ada

Furthermore, I wish I could shave but once
near a dogwood, swim the Mississippi up close
& personal then bury my body in a pact

with the devil, come anew as the fallen limb
floating past the bridge. In the car wheeling east
someone said a brilliant word, its rotation

lost between the lit splendor of these hills
& plains. Always the anger of hardheaded men
but that billboard's our rearview, yesterday

if we're lucky. We're lucky, upshift toward
miles of reverie & for the span of a pasture
I back into the boyish arms of the Willamette,

river I call home, call breathless, even call
deep & curled as though by her kiss. In Subiaco,
we kill the engine for the fabled poet's grave,

search until we find the stone named Francis
(whispering Frank) & refuse to let his life
spark voiceless into the earth. Our country

over half these dozen days begins to shrink,
every step swung &, stage left, the understudy
trills & hums from the mailbox to a door

that yawns & lets the morning in. This spins
like vinyl, lowers the needle into its Big River,
its Old Blue, flips that record until a voice

emboldens our own. When I insist to speak
I implore the air, wager the home on my shoulder
that I might never lose this music for the single,

wide-open gaze when at last the fluent water
greets the sea. When I insist on meaning,
this one lives inside a riverbank, this one strokes

ever farther from its shore. I wish I didn't even
bear remorse, wave goodbye to the weather
& each flood where it leaves the body's mouth.

Taking Your Half of the Middle

The closing phrase should read god help me
when I hurry back from the ancient songs

ringing my head all day, those loved & those
unwittingly lost as I press forth regardless,

reclaim a childlike marvel & focus on the cloth
balled beneath the rush of our kitchen tap,

heft & the shape like some rare heart, then use
that irregular fabric to remove my boy's face,

I mean his menageries of crackers & berries
where they fall below & the moon of my nails

waning, less white, nearsighted & no excuse
for in due course I'm dying as much as anyone,

like a magnet whenever a memory of our cat
saunters forward & through the sunlit door

where a calendar turns, a refrigerator opens
&, because now I've mentioned it, I'm craving

diamonds of melted butter, the golden crust
scrumptious & when I see that final threshold

allow me first to whistle down my childhood
street, find that a glass of familiar ice awaits,

bends the light for a piece of bread my brother
told me was every meal inside a prison cell,

crumbs & water & enough that I demanded
my life like a hymn, my Sunday best & praying

I might discover a lasting faith, leave behind
those restless fears of each recited blessing

forsaken, dark calamity between that if-I-die
& before-I-awake, so long my toys to the box,

best friends to lesser friends, my ladybugs
to the airtight jar, even parents to the earth

from which time & again our cat swaggers,
tucks himself in the daffodils & eyes the feeder,

wellspring for any season & should the seeds
fail, or the apples roll clear from the table,

let us bow, fill our mouths before those fruits
couple chance to reason, gloom into green

when the seagulls pitch & begin their circling
somewhere above a parking lot, over fields

& like a dream in which these skies open up,
pouring rains soak the yard & yes, god help us.

Amarillo Catches Fire in the Distance

Naturally sky & red, the one compared to summer
leaves, blown across the street & what was I
supposed to say searching stoves, up old homes
over the fence & down. My belt broke sometime
Californian, the power steering gone not forgotten,
nothing muscle couldn't muster or absorb. Swallowed
my gum for pygmy love inside the indie rock club.

Mileage on the hips & the lake swayed. Gawking,
more awful each discomfort & the male gaze
three-for-a-dollar with your preferred member
super saver discount card. In robust description,
my wonderful, homely time was dry & I knew
not what I wanted, whatever coming to my mouth
coming also closer to the heart. Smooth move, ex-lax.

This weather still flits, smirking, & Portland heeds
my jokes, no random affection when I recall sweeping
our porch in the rain. So far the tenor straight-
forward, leaps lacking longevity as if written down,
notebooks brown to keystrokes. In Texas, well,
in Texas. Missouri stood in the hall where the radio
played. From his desk, Will said the towers were dust.

Chicago & nearly December, I erred a final nethering,
former things taped & sealed though I imagined yet
stopping for gas, snacks, stretch the treadmill
mood & low-lying visions of family night. Various
breeds of same, hurtling in space both curious
& routine, then for once cropping a somber wing
off someone other than other people. Oh what in me
rose no greater than an umbrella, what in me stank.

Some dire lessons in Eugene, the landlord drubbing
every tree & we cried without hesitation, thinking
bubbles in the blood. No, I did not forget you
nor suffering, back on my knees inside the wood
we personified, shook, later blowing the sugar shack
dry in New England. Matchstick, infer smithereen
or the numberless days we beckoned the river & lived.

Postmarked naturally in Idaho & the city this troop
calls like wallpaper home, pattering on lids & the close,
elbow comfort of friends. By this I'm the nest of bad
situations, eyes accordioned but my mind's off
when the shot glass trips. I could use a new basket
as my handle cracked, traffic such a mess we say
cursed, still in our best parts, yesterday & tomorrow.

In the Time of Sandpaper & Roses

I know your tears, where they used to sleep
& perhaps I'm no more glum than a child
yet born, unconscious yet tethered & trailing
its ship set to sail. The oceans surrender
our test results &, after that, bottles bring
messages cavernous, memorized, thirsty.
I'm no more my self-winding fist, no doubt
drifting where strings of a gorgeous hat go
when the wave dissolves everything, erasing
even queens speedy on their feet but not
sped enough. One must feed to flourish,
not the husband ebbed high into the limbs
after a week of floods, now days of humidity.
The oceans say I've a daughter behind me,
flowers directly & blind. The oceans say
you see me wading grass, danger to myself,
etcetera. I wanted adoration, famous & hung
to the wall. Instead I'm wads of gum, spent
& stuck, become one with she who stuck it
there. Of heaven & betrayal, let's replay
too often being left for that other for good.
Mornings when you hear the many dying feet
leap across my head, strange infancy curls
as though in a stove. I have that wherewithal

still, I've my few friends & still I have you.
I take to the streets, to rainfall, to the pools.
They are oceans & I dream we're improving.

MUSEUM OF THE DEPARTED

—for Capron

When you are a face & slipping this & that way
apart, when a trench again replaces a thought
out of which jokes rise, laughter to be exact
& sharp, closing on the skin. Cómo se dice

my bag ripped, shattered a tall jar of olives,
ordinary loss startling, nudged oncoming
& sudden this way? Listen to the words, actors
worn or everyone leaning in regret too well

& it's trying to bluff us inevitably as Lucy
yanking the ball that Charlie hustles to kick,
swings instead through air. What goes up
makes many splendid views from then & there

where the cold satellites float on their faces
looking down, us little ones with a mortal bug
touched, staring back. I looked from that height
years away, specific days becoming decades

hardly visible now for the fog, some speck
once noted &, once viewed, unavoidably
darkening our room. In this corner dandelion,
damnation of the dreaming things possible

& still with my jacket removed under the heat,
laid out to deny the puddle its beloved's feet
who am I kidding: chivalry, dilly-dallying
then eating it too. Let me try this again, this

notion like sleep that no more keeps a friend
or foe, the black & white beagle everyone says
needs putting down. The dream chews gum,
with another's phone takes pictures, with some

scrambles in upright ways to tear the goalposts
free. You taught me to strum down down up,
up down & we talked the good shit. I'd say
these things no longer matter if I didn't better

know the ache toting groceries home. It's over
but it's been fun, apparitions under the door
& expecting its latch to hold as I hold the moon
waxing as you die, now in Christmas fullness

much less so without you singing to rivers,
body that could've rung anywhere but chose to
here, might for all we know surface yet alive,
might be the earth, oxygen & dirt, ir-re-fucking-

placeable. The pine trees prefer their roots
not show & never worry how the ending comes
or that the sky bears a pall if the pall dampens
winter, its musty sweater when the furnace

burns through its fuel. It doesn't make much,
much sense, yellow bird to flutter a lifetime
not so often the one you think or wanted,
preferring to cut the rug deep into the night,

days crawling before they toddle the curb,
grass & sidewalks near little flags to let us know
what's buried underneath. Limb & blossom,
leaving when finished so others might sit

one by one hurrying with the honeycomb
knocked forever from its branch, small home
in the eaves. In mumbling weather & patter
all lines lead to last in line, linens lead to what

I offer awake, light of the open fridge an hour
& two. My friend is dead, won't pretend the sun
burst through the rain, won't the easy image
making meaning as there's none, no why

alongside silence in this horseshit debate,
this horseshit, this horseshit when Linus wants
his blanket over the shoulder, lost but once
before lifting a thumb out of here. The caption

lands where no compadre reads it & the day
still says hello, remains calm, finds vistas
hard to say & half introduces each stranger
by the name of he who became the shadow,

photograph, the lately emptied bar. These
& other voices come to me, shaking my hand,
tugging my heels. I'd like memory to wake him
tonight, drive for the horizon kind of thing

saying hello to San Francisco, hello to Oakland,
traffic, ugh. I don't know water well or why
acceptance must polish grief. Here I want
my friend swirling old in conversations,

waiting as I stop to tie my shoe or strum
down down up, up down, down down up,
up down for the burning day. I want to trust
our bodies will ripple in wondrous, new places.

Paysage Triste

—January 20, 2017

Much sorrow to be, oh how lovely to be
loved, unsaid & undone before a wave
doles out its visible pang, come now

this woe unto me & splayed. Why not
prospects, whistling out past clouds
beneath which I drove & maybe me too

dumb, stowaway in the trunk's dark well
asking by match for decades long faded
& crumbs. A cowboy plays president,

paws a jelly bean dish while we boys lust
blind, skinniest attention & all aglow,
A-B-Cs to matriculation. I'd like to say

Lord & Savior, but my better horse says
best be careful, to be alone & unfetter
my feet each from their wearied buckets,

harbor not the bent bulk of heartbreak
& reason. Animals, a lifetime ago & now
out of which I must address that man

doting on hems, oh those hobnobbers
gladly notching yet another featherhead
into the trunk of a tree, a weedy hair

no bird would collect in the bare century
relieved, leafless. My country tumbles,
moreover stalls in standing a woman

to steer, blind instead & swaggering
with men who say oh-I'd-never but vow
no one in a dress deserves the blessing,

buh-bye, back into the mire. Lovely,
we boys proudly men, elbowing in & out
like air, holding the door & collecting

smiles until we're pleased. Oh why not
damning bedamned, waver & blight
berated & why not name the ruptures

slurred by the smug middle of the heart
until we heed, at last, common sense
& swerve off this vulgar bridge for good.

Fear of Drowning

Like ten thousand fibers the sky lets down
her hair, the cats & dogs, gophers & geraniums,
cohorts all & to what do I owe the leisure of my ear
paired with the cloud unhinged, the drum
rolling out a thunderstorm. I'm stranger in town
having drunk like a fish, eaten like a bear, once more
slurred like I've an inkling toward delight &,
somehow, alive this side of morning. Last night,
ten curious toes afloat in the pool, I forgot
how much I want to sink to that very bottom
& stay, how the prints left over the tile & into bed
remind me of saplings planted single file, even
how they grow into fine things before falling
expelled. If life ended now how do I, how dare I
complain for my lot, from the yonder curb
stealing the pinecone larger than any known fist,
tossing it back with the luggage & thinking maybe
my daughter can love this. As I can't steer the erratic,
ongoing mind, not beyond some other season
yielding corn & swollen by the wind our bodies trail,
I want to know who lends a shelter, who a river
that weaves between the flame of memory
& so many friends. If a life shutters, if it dreams
no hereafter for a muddled eye, then onward

deep into the fountain & me still believing it good
choosing how we shed this world, forget music
to sleep like grass or chrysanthemum. In a given day
you try finding a thing or two worth stopping for
& do, despite holes shot through the scenery
where not even one primrose resides. This is life,
tattered & obscure, tempting the book closed
once guessing its end. In a straight path anyway,
I release the umbrella & its faultless, dripping
curves, blossom & shine & where to go next
after falling on a single, hopeful note long as I can

.

Forever Is Composed of Nows

When I think all's lost, washed or better
over, I milk what's new to sing, find manner
& mind its rules. I like T.V. too, always believed
fences between "it feels good" & "I love you."

It feels good. I love you fat as butter,
your hat & matching charm, the cursory fork
without stabbing our eyes. Mirror mirror,
sleek as satin on the wall & wills of those I loved
broken, smelling of an outhouse & I, eternal
nitwit. I ate my heaping bowl of sunshine
this morning. You try it, you like nuts
& bolts in perpetuity, sanitized, & then arrive
to witness the reenactment of a crime.

Sleep grins as if on the dentist's shoulder,
plastic the grocer wears for a coat & the beard
merely spares my chin. Ceiling fans swim,
I drop trout to argue a thing still stands a thing
by its past, suffering a tragic sweater…

Excusez-moi, I peeped a pure direction
& detour by train. I'll need a haircut never,
no more shaves. That old man roars handsomely,
tenders snow, & the orange that sways
& shimmies between his shoes… I'm sure
it's jolly as all get out. I'm sure it'll bring us joy.

GOODNIGHT WHOEVER YOU ARE

Must be a gift to shrug what others shoulder,
what's blown from the rooftop & nonetheless
asleep, not I swear another flooded forfeit,

catalogue of a poor magician staged & reciting
daily harm, run-of-the-mill regret. Evenings
I read a thing or two on Mozart, cause of death

unknown or working yet as a janitor in Nebraska
where he paces under rain. If I turn yesterday
I'm a ghost, nothing myself. Maybe a ninny,

blue & motley, rolling the tired semicircle
sidewise in a plastic August breeze, three sheets
& away with the wind. When the barflies quit,

quake & sweat or when the one besets the other
my good eye wins, tracks twice to the window
against which a future checks its teeth, waits

& behind the beveled glass imagines marriage,
pledge & fruit of every American billboard,
then finally knocks. I'd nothing brainy to say

(Nebraska, oh I mean Amherst), stood anyway
as if the fields knew my trade. Faceless hills,
lamps of summer in galaxy gray, we touch & go

toward war like a thousand birds, apparent death
before the engines howl & lift a chimney brick
or recover from the splash with a fish. It falls

now to the neighbors & only later did we leave
ill-manner in water, walk without remembering
each echo of a rusted trampoline, bedspring

& washing machine, the conversation held years
where we planted feet like we'd stay, pleased
our umbrella didn't cartwheel past the yard

overgrown in firefly & thicket both. We crested
like a wrongheaded tune, flickered & nodding
& knowing that touch & go meant Massachusetts,

home, a surfeit of skunks for who can really say
how many afternoons will gnaw our corners,
our resolve along the bumper-to-bumper cars

foiled & sunk. Twice today that low wisdom
moved the horizon, swept me near the exit
like kisses flare, like tinder inhales & everyone

thinks nothing but fire. I rouse to the credits
casual & free, merge with the midday shine
raising a finger to the temple, my ready thumb

tempted among the shadows gone, & their trees.

The Odd Ring of Reality

Continuing on your marks, by the summer
finished when traffic clots midmorning
still &, later, toward big homes or a jet-skied
gravy lake. Soon enough the barrels steam,
lying-in-wait decades climb, somersault
that otherwise empty womb. Up to where
paint meets the trim I stare, my greed that is
turning out the light. It was morning long
before we met & will be again, now & again.
Every three seconds someone in this city
commits a selfie. There another one fallen
from that big red bridge off to the west
& on the train passing by I sometimes move
to better, more fully face those wrinkles
waiting behind a clumpy bush, the twisting
new tree that doesn't burn over just any
little shake of waning thought. I nearly
hear the bottles cleaned, can't throw them
for nothing & barely mention the sword
between the back & forward beat marked
within my red mind. This gives me pleasure,
as they say: yesterday the zoo's vacant cage
yet depicting flowers, boulders well-plastered,
savannah far as I could see. Some weekends

I'd rather bed among the small- to petty-sized
stones, cold styrofoam as the people come
then go, come then go. Of course too I'd
happily follow by the thick & thin, claim
every posture in the wending line my own.
I have arrows & a borrowed bow, lessons
& whatever facts remain. I can venture to say
that cow but yonder even looks like a cow.

Paint by Numbers

Out from the cockcrow the news hurries in
&, if the recent dead watch over us, then
we scratch in company the days, even at rest

under the elongated light of a digital clock,
salmon-like. Salmon & apricot & a voice
presuming something's wrong, why nothing

made up in paper cups playing telephone
& the message of a man, his ticking now dim,
divisible, muffled & still the match struck,

desks & tables to block his path. Always a man
muscling doorway to hallway to some prone,
expectant room, not a monarch of anything

but sick as if plugged with wax. Always a man
weighing heavily a score, his heel for years
slipped off the curb into plots of yellow tape

& the splintering glass, vain, garden-variety
this desire to be touched, leaning to the spigot
then finding its cool water drained. Not faith

exactly, nor the command from heaven if ever
there was, but the starlight in aquamarine,
that hour like an engine purring & becoming

yet this incessant trill tuned for a bell, cower
& cover, no one for a sneeze replying bless you
just the man. Always a man & the lucky ones

insisting it couldn't happen here, no cloud
stealing a student in her chair, a teacher in his
plea & stutter. Or rather relief when a man,

just a man walks in & asks to borrow the pencil
or pen, a stapler or this very sheet of paper,
its fiber of the everyday & nothing more to fear,

not even a man bent on becoming the cold
coward of a snake. A snake & its urging done.
It wasn't so bad. It won't even hurt until it does.

THE BEREFT ROBOTICS OF THE SOUL

Scraps of summer, of the leftover world
framed by low-risen, hip-steadying
coffee on the early train, tiny speakers in each
inadvertent shiver denying the ear. Strange,

contagious rupture & returning to it
(you're welcome) that crowd bumps me joyous
& like contracted sky, like blue unthinkables
collapsed, capsized, merely happening.

I used to fly but don't believe further ridings
or the objects reappearing in a distance
my mirrors do reverse. Their skewbald past
even now, faces a face meets & fractions

each one late in reacting, knowing no
pure formulation before the light escapes
& stops. The ribbon unknots, so with it
its balloon I tried to retrieve, rewind, oh dear.

Seems the be-all & end-all of nothing huddles
maudlin in the fringe. Of particular parties
I love the reparable glow, somethin-ing someone
silken & allergic. On intimacy this leans,

lastly between my arms, their burden stung
& their oughts, their gonna-be-over-soons
pinning my poor memory in place, skulduggery
white, what a lily apology couldn't undo.

Takes an ample dimwit to visit former spaces
slurred, rewriting the tale over mornings,
mornings, mornings. I loved the wilds clarified,
each toying the wall, their actual leaves

blowing dark a candle at such & such an address,
from the room its otherworldly inhabitants
not wishing all of it again. Instead at ease,
smitten in the newfangled age, with being alive.

You Know It's Nearly Spring

Even as you pedal & rave, muscle ever closer
toward your eighth birthday, the gardens
flower crocus here & there through winter

around the block, upset with rain. Enough fool-
hardy heart, curious pilot for what it often wants,
spreading mayo on this or that & the weather

too impassioned for snow, the five-day forecast
louder than volume up from a toy that stalls,
steals the stray lace you're tying (your damnedest)

thirty-three years later, one foot worn as the first
& straightaway lulled, pins & needles asleep
beneath the leg of your old kitchen chair. This,

like any perfected skill, speaks in low-budget
diction, hence divides its time snatching towels
to necking on a yellow bus. Such itches burn out,

recuse themselves from the everyday tit-for-tat
tug-of-war between the what-do-you-thinks
& the what-were-you-thinkings. No doubt many

doldrums land in the wake of swimming bottles,
slamming doors, or the spark starting to blaze
into a much happier life. Or like a child's romance

authentic, now shuttered, so the lucky summer
your head insists slow-witted, puerile, nonetheless
buzzing while here again March, here in April

& with it aiming to be someone who didn't
hesitate, will not surprise when the letter says,
Sorry about your loss. Hardly a wink to rehearse,

begin to love a shadow where the trophy hung
like a holy relic, before it woke one morning
nameless, sublime, outright in a plastic alley can.

People You May Know

—for Dan Chelotti

I, too, dumbfounded by it, exquisite
beyond the glass where the bird drapes
fluttered & done, discarded thing

& its silence yet annunciating the proud month,
months gone. In gallant afterthought
I, fledgling, darted by train, forth in time

reading snowmelt & throwaway cups,
cars holding earshot of the churn as the engine
couples, reverses direction. I close

my books to better elicit the lined fence,
collect tranquil folk in lawn chairs
all but forgotten. Within this weather

it browns, irrefutable maples & bare scrub
deciding the day. With a suitcase
sidestepping along, through the shade

darkening my wits & this valley alike,
I'm stranger to Amherst, yet to block its sun
& circling planes. A dollar in my pocket,

hand amnesic & pretending anything
but abandoned, likely tattered, surely haunted,
older than its brother. When I hitch,

I wrestle flowers to gift my name a summer
thawed green. When time hurries
next to marry landscape, the humidity

that occupies nook & cranny dilates
far as decent eyes can see. The town is actual,
skies purring more blue than postcards

or a sailor's suit. The surrounding wood
comes back prized, bountiful, three coughs
later & turned inside, outside rather

if I'm healthy & occasion twists an arm,
no funny stuff alongside the Unitarian church,
over cracks with electric hum. Places

everyone, smooth brows & just below them
constellations licked, particulars
lost to tiny, visible fires. I think it's July,

high-sounding. Soon it's September where
(long past the pharmacist, the jeweler,
chop-chop cheerio the fraternity, split couches

flaccid with Greek) I'm embracing friends
thataway, brooms to lean in our ears,
bumping matches off dandelions

useful yet by their storied, gray heads
& foxes we misread as loping dogs, ferrying
campus squirrels yonder for the pond

or athletic fields we'll never careen, not
even when pink mystery at sundown
abounds. Powdery shafts of incandescence,

the same gangly pack, no no we chew
too many words, jumping through the window
in lieu of a door. We stutter half circles

around the poet's fervent, unclouded hand,
we trip over his typewriter to catch
its mind, globes of his own coinage & we

do not confess quickly, sure as hell
some dream for which no one hankers,
how its browns only stand bright

among the peripheral leaves, autumn
unnoticeable as the neighbors until behind us,
complete, good riddance. I'd like to say

we cannot buy the rumor of a steeple
sunk beneath the Quabbin. I'm susceptible
like others, over & misheard kissing

(small attempts), kisses between pages
& nervy canoodles unbeknownst,
garbled & dizzy, the forever staircase

holding a wink our trysts with the moon,
our waltzing. There must be rousing, inevitable
surges & late birdcalls as gravediggers

belt down their beers. I'd like to say
better now than never to the unclouded hand
you are a father & incomparable. You'd

eat an elephant for lunch, one parched foot
thirsting another. You pantomime
soap & razor across your chin's horizon

where hawks multiply, carriages roll
babies through bald hills, seventeen lanes
bound in jet skis, the lake village,

a tree, pneumatic tree parading readily
& toward the parlor mirror that flickers a wave
or wellspring or cascade. Afternoons

contract & lengthen in yellow swimwear
on the shore, kiddos invariably lacing
sneakers for a contest, thwacking

balls atop the woodpile, the challenge
"always to find the ultimate in the ordinary
horseshit." After the weekend & its vulgarities,

you paint the mind a lily. White's the rage,
free as air & the charcuterie board
courtesy of our chef, don't mention it

nor the little finger like a language raised
curbside, warning shot across Main
& North Pleasant streets, beyond the gates

behind the filling station where stones
replace sky, where Emily sleeps
after a honeyed chase. You & yours

to decorate her grave stash a clip-on toy,
ten-cent crown, the parachute of a retired stiff
nestled unscathed, wry on the branch

up up & lustrous at the end of one season,
blocks of ice breezing into town
before we even recognize their clothes,

schoolbooks numb in their bellies,
chalky halos, aboard-about-above in a cursive
neglected. With dozing lectures, sure,

but no murder. Erase too the slow bus
of backyard arborists, curls silver
& moral. Plus the police on their bicycles,

however many tickets roosting, unseen
till it's mums for the Volvo wagons
buried in the snow. The unabridged troupe

at their X's, paramour of the open library
shushing her mocha & that son of the "famous"
so & so peddling vinyl, no poet himself

nor desirous to wait before the postmistress
who bids our envelopes a fine farewell,
passage snug & never suggesting

corpses, unspeakables in the tobacco barn
rejected for abusing the preposition. A gauntlet
thrown down, scattered fights against

literalists lacking fortitude & who thank you
for the opportunity, wish you the best
placing it somewhere else. Luckily,

despite the stars, a river, the mouthfuls
flowing variable, I fidget imagination
& it renders, approachably greens so forget

the brouhaha, its bouquet & the tongue
under April rain. Been there, tasted
days sprouting, "the ones that can be saved"

& upon their knees, no shoes no shirt no
kidding, bang bang the brain extinct, heavenly
brain. Cloverleaves are yawning,

insolence & its parsimonious smoke arrives
& disappears like a ghost. The evidence
(titmice times three) hints this tally might've

happened in a hammock. I'm the veteran now,
running his nose across the sleeve, my
high-fevered binoculars leveled

for inspection of a hot slice at Antonio's,
new blood rising over the shoulder, tuft of hair
zigzagging the lower lip. Regrets, a few

but then I'd wed again in a heartbeat
this stranger, parade my mason jar of pennies
flattened on the track. The train whistles,

it blinks & blows out a harmless nightmare
where the bear five-fingers the hummingbirds
their feeder. By my damnedest I don't

knock stone at the unacquainted future,
deadhead a daffodil. I'm susceptible
like others & admit the raft floating down

the Connecticut, its substance relished
& swirling. To the unclouded hand
life's ducky, thank you for asking,

your common armchair sits nothing short
of a god, I swear. For a manyeth time
I load my canteen, compulsory tear-jerking

(all indelicacy) while outside the flags sail,
half dance or snooze. In their shadow,
by their indifferent symbols, I dub my escape

sub rosa & starting bent with the morning mail
toward a lamp that echoes its treetop tune
easy on the eyes, cool enough to sip,

that which nips the interior some good
nine hundred western miles later. Trying
not to balloon as I could the sultry

solicitations, doorways & enigmatic
smiles, I paw this ashy earth. Overhead,
chickadees in orbit, what remains

genuine. In ready, permissive hindsight,
I flipped my magnet past the bison pastures,
goats tame & from the town I loved,

the unclouded hand yet loved. Absolute &
trembling, I stared hard across a prairie
called Toledo, Ohio, & I hauled like a pioneer.

WHILE YOU WERE OUT

After touting the wall no ladder can climb,
my non-ironic double drains his beer,
pegs the housekeeping shady. By night
& like a moth it's always someone
risking the northbound interstate,
drinking if not from the well of tire swings
then from the eyes of a sleeping bird.

Shy of yellow, our sunny-side eggs
temper cold. Around the corner
& there, to your right, the elevator sticks
to its second story, one in which terror
evokes the good old, golden days...

When we're kids chasing fireflies, no gate
needed a latch. We thought the stars
no more than marbles warming the sky.

The spotlight, white, bids a white crowd
& burdock roots where it wouldn't
yesterday. Against some whisper
filching already a polycotton off his back,
my non-ironic double hears America
open-mouthed, flaring, her carols unvaried.

Today in the Whale

Tail over teakettle if my boy didn't pitch
duly, electrodes spiked in two sets of waves
& horrible, his heart foiling a metronome
like thousands of buoyant ants less quick
than the ocean where we wish they'd row
their heads, the thorax, their abdomens.
His sister says, Don't let a crocodile eat you
& we cut breath, pace shore to later shore
through trombones & a hubbub of news
horned across the charts, a papery thought
between doctors & doctors. Never were we
immune to splendor or hope or saying, Damn
that moon, let not a sliver reverse its shine
or meddle in the middle of our private wars.
In a word, if anything's true dinosaurs are not
real. Except for a sea star. Except for sharks
& bees & when their toothy harvest comes
I simply want our boy to live. His hazel eyes
skip & browse, he scoots the sunlight now
despite such scenes I imagined & suffered
without him, curtains instead of the pictures
we'd someday straighten in the playroom
like plastic ants, a wound nose, rubber pigs
I'd teach him to hide as my teachers taught me

during visits to the town's famous grave
& not for an ordinary, wasted life, no sunset
slipped past the horizon & our downcast,
lacking correctives. For a heart beating fast
such syringes prodded, lunged & missed until
his mother left the room, found no corner,
not even the distant corridor free of our boy's
almighty bellow. I nearly begged the gods,
there & then, held him snug to better know
his goodness, to resist losing my druthers
over a child whose song breaks open my chest.

Carved in the Tree of My Neighbor's Backyard

Call it another gift, losing your keys so we could find them
by doorways bricked shut, our sure movements rubbing
mortar & its clustered joints with each corner nudged
until all remains shaken, stirred. About a rectangle ghost

my new lens over an older model dimmed, tools of the trade
better described as mentors, dedicated friends & maybe
we haven't spoken, will not have that illuminated chance
& therefore the baby crawls for a bottle across the floor,

so many definite articles where his offing bends forever
forming questions, e.g. fathers & their little deaths before us,
more concretely my own father revived in gasoline smell,
genie from its nozzle, knuckled hose & click. Each time

I feel his hunger I drain another pint of water or look up
sparrows on the new feeder all aggressive, territorial
pissings in the backyard of here. I've told this before, no?
I've told you already of men swinging near, how they inch,

steer, then take the hearts of everyone & specifically where
no one knows. They refuse sweeps of marriage & death
& how the latter lasts too entirely long. I want to say
how the brilliance of some I loved looked suddenly gray

when they hurried the field. I've told you in a rumor mill
I should've rung from within my shell, head over heels
toward the concave self, refresh-my-mail-go-to-sleep, wake,
check the tended memory. Viewpoint extended on a stick

ad infinitum, ad nauseam rising high the me, you & everyone
before disappearing like powder in a glass, forget me yet
letting the teardrops roll down. If I think of the warmest day
I see the sun & a raincloud licked inside that same library,

more likely the same book. It's a fourth printing, happy
to be & not a dark spot on the downside of the canyon wall
or some endless summer when I searched the drawers
& closets, hoping for a single glove my child might wear

to reappear. If I confess the plain vulnerability, silly me,
in that instant I flush, rush to finish before my children cry
or wake, or clean a little up before those little whiles
when I'd be the flinch beneath the fireworks that were,

too often, my father in the driveway. His intention floats
& surely I've said my own lifts a hand from the spigot,
fingers opening before the water reaches my lips, floods
instead the ground where, somehow, a yellow flower grows.

Meeting the Middle Western Day

He watches the first flashing car chase a second
left & right by degrees along the rug, circled

like a red crayon around the window's frame
from a day or two now gone. Beyond glass,

departures blur the prairie hour where my city
flutters in the sun, reel of birdseed & chitter,

chimneys of pip. Back inside, my boy's balloon
volleys curious, hops on heat out the furnace,

connects dapples between sounds as if the heart
already hollers, belting open its mouth, thick

& awkward. How my appetite for leave-taking
throbs, foxtrots & beelines & nevertheless it

lags behind what coils out the pistol's muzzle
before it too lands speechless. A curious thing

struck time again in the head by a stuffed tiger,
odds of my boy's life said better than those south

or on the west side, likelier to receive sparrows
than take the bearing of a dozen brass casings,

flicker I almost compare with flurry & feather
here in the repeated footage of the dash cam

but vanishes instead in failure of the boy's arms
both, neck & bone. Sirens drift from my easy

eavesdrop, mind swift to festoon & accordingly
slipped into the backing of the lifeguard nest,

last season's sand burying our salt-weary feet
while motley beach umbrellas uproot, stumble

& leap with the sun as ever stretched like a yawn
over castles & bottle caps, threatening to warm

out from nowhere seals &, along the waterline,
therein joined & staring up as if for direction

by my city's dead young boys. The balloon pops,
sirens alarm & sprawl but, inside, it's all milk

streamed into coffee to soften the brightening
hue of the room, whims that mimic a fever,

resemble a second body within my body roused
& beginning to peck. Up off elbows & knees,

my boy doles food in the metal bowl then trails
our dog, tilts & stalls, hung in middle flight

unlike the bullet, until he falls & loosens his belly
& grins. My child lusts for the nonstop circuits

airplanes tend to make, tacks thrill to each ball
& relaying moon lulled by its own weight down,

loves his mother's lactating flesh, yes, & coins
plunked in pools & piggybanks. He prizes clocks,

O's of otter & Ohio when the brimmed trooper
let us off, me without the thought of broken

limb or rib, tested trigger or a bloodied brow,
only the inklings of everyday mileage ahead

& bypassing the obvious, credit the accident
or chance or coincidence & not my privileged,

for-no-good-reason skin. How much radiance
wanders blind when I scroll numb the latest

body camera darted & done, thereafter feeding
my son blueberries, forgetting even the shadows

dawn casts over him? My boy's young enough
to be held, to nestle wide-eyed with his ear

bent to another's chest, trot an unpunctuated
glee for the plush of a pillow, ordinary blankets

scattering the floor. I watch him watch the car
chase a second as if their return might keep

from happening. Oh the rounds I like to knock,
set them with music & so arrange my course

repeating a phrase over & again, over & again
until there appears a grace, cosmic gratefulness

that bends the answer out of hunger & believes
love alone can lift a body from the bullet's air,

apples from the worm, relief from the endings
sparrows still cut through boys. In the new year,

naked, my city illuminates its skyline, tallies
from zero its foul play, hands into the hundreds

uplifted as though to release a tiding difficult
& bare, windfall of light into the advancing day.

Before It's a Memory It's a Photograph

Less a formal feeling & more how lovely anyplace
with thee, Ada dubs us the band back together,
laughter in fact pulled as though one of us wasn't all
ah-hem, guys, I'm standing right here. In Raleigh,
heaps of houses remind me of Emily Dickinson,
splintered, antique mirrors called in a culmination
back. You needn't patience nor meet the lens
having been there, kneeling on the carpet or leaning
enough to know bad choices then make them
nonetheless. Wild nights, evidently, & in the AM
thus a phone's ill-starred news, clothes packed
& scatter. Dickinson lived here, there, & over here
(forget me not) I elbow the glass, shards innumerable
where another you chases a paddle & upstream
sleeps on islands, the nearly anodyne affair accruing
seven, eight & nine beers gone. I'm doodled,
as if a bird on whom I could've hinted something
hasn't collywobbled null & void. I guess I'm rotten
thinking my stamina 2003 instead of on clearance,
learning yet to steal a poem, how best to feed it
& keep the whole thing alive without smoking albeit
our curbs show otherwise. We could use a broom
steady, steady now in the Polaroid, on t-shirts
or bantered like Redford out of focus & sinking boats,

everything's crowning oh, I'm sorry… You too
should've been there & not the far end of the table
smiling maybe never. Honestly, I'd a pen in my pocket
& now peddle pencils to the flattered, rented page,
renderings in which you wouldn't erase anything
from Casey, Patrick footing the feast not even
Eric saw it coming but agrees we should launch
our own bar with a jukebox grumbling the one band
we love to hate. We know, like white on white,
every word committing what we promised to forget
or is it that other way, egregiously a face or two
& next to nothing, no one, nowhere dappled
outside last call. I poured midsentence then rife,
above our bourboned heads the futile, unrepentant
curve of moon. Tonight your town's so… You're
like an angel & I'm… Unmoored, hearts rowing
or we'd spin forever the compass & together
wake in early light, over our heels & downstairs
yawning like lions tawny, benign, terrifyingly still.

CROSSING PONTCHARTRAIN

Impulse breathes good morning & another
replies with a nod. For even a gentle tap,

knuckle & smile on the far side of the glass
I'm grateful. For what measures whole,

what equals scrap & especially for the sky,
its village of clouds & the heavenly distance

lit, majestic before the unforeseen road
& likewise touching the fence. Thank you

tussles & inconceivable nests, hatchlings
between the spout & a hard place. Impulse

to be reborn, to improve our various selves
when a day spurs speed & snaps, contracts

across our tongues. Credit as well the good
in looking, to fail at lifting a source of joy,

mispronouncing the birds, thimbles & trees
more green than in a photograph. Impulse

for pollen, yes pollen, its accountable dusts
& sneezes we interrupt the hour to bless,

catalyst & shiver, bare shoulders of the valley
& the sultry gorge. For each & every sum

my thanks for your shimmer & bask, impulse
inviting the river while the next summons

its shore. Impulse for swimming, turned on
full, zeniths of our bodies to greet the sun

& thanking too the eye of language, a circle
of contact blushing buoyant, feeding itself

cheek to cheek for more impulse on its way,
speaking of what reveries surround this all

like air. Without a pause, with the fleeting
impulse not to give thanks but then I do

for the traces of gold, grace, impulse yet seen
oh my friends, one & all, friends pulsating

fearless & late, our affections inseparable,
whistling, shaking love, spilling out in praise.

As I Bow & Pass Smiling

Lone, pensive limb among the other
limbs in the opening air
among things, I make myself free
weekdays eight to five. This is this moment
my life awaits & it's much like the ring
of last year. Look, I sigh & only to myself.

Three winds & the millennium,
coolness rushed I remember that. Digging
tangles of a yard &, later, the spade
at Williams' gray stone, behind
his wooden walls the desk. It's like the dead
& collapse of their charms, the sprout
who leans to captain a model boat
called the Coral Reef. & the trunkfish caught

but mostly, inside a carnation,
some knock-down, drag-out fighting
by the ghost of a bee. I too am mortal, woke
like a leaf on the wet glass, pretty please
versus pretty pleased. Deduction tells me
instances are strewn with seagulls,
& for a backdrop the hangman's knot.

Then again was the funniest conundrum
the other day. Again were margins
like squirrels or the fox reflected in my
if-I-ever-donned-them shades. Thus I think little
for holes that needle & hoodwink the sky.

Russian Thistle & Other Items of Note

High between windows like waves or spent cloud
look, I'm here & young or you're old & parallel
aiming our phones for no reason other than being

or that some in the city have never seen prairie
no, no shred of what it is. Fake it or leave it, I fail
willing a weekend wild, no likes nor a karma instant,

my status becoming in time a mint face unfriended
like these zero sums without emoji, the whatever
public bouquets & hoping there exists a healing

I'd click impulsively, one-click repeatedly & willful
I guess. At best the familiar, dense voice struggles
to keep a tone forever, meaning until tomorrow

afternoon. Maybe in the next life, another day
in yours & felt if saying so myself, looking how I lit
tumbleweed to brighten what I thought the dead

couldn't know, what they shouldn't. Minus weed,
we used sandwich bags & glue. I loved to watch
cherry trees or even sneakers strung over the wires,

stoic flowers & words stuttered like Henry Ford's
catch & crank, then I'd leap as if the straightforward
matures in a single day. Matisse made oil in 1951,

so there. In 1997 a blue gust frisked my pocket
& in it the twenty-dollar gaze of Andrew Jackson
became merely a speck for the sky, such gratuitous

gumption to have believed I knew some little bit
through neighborhoods & barrooms & the kids
wandering by chewing gum. I'd the basics of bases,

their relation to necking, grazing breasts, etcetera,
know it now as what-I-did among boys & for the girls
what-was-done-to-me. While a good many doted

freedom & trails, I swam three Oklahoman nights
within my martini, panoraming for gravity fails,
back-to-school fails, top ten fails, each oh my god

when the warbler broke indelibly the glass reflection
of a star. Hidden, a backpack more than anything
wishes to paint the faraway, celebrating crowds

framed in faraway streets. In its wake a kindliness
propositions, repairs the split blossoms to keep them
alive & longer. We slip our bodies, the tidal surge

makes landfall, pushes inland to steal from the heart
its proper noun. All the more reason to awaken,
greet the light, fasten knots to our real world shoes.

STUDY OF COFFEE, NICOTINE, & PAPER

—for James Foley

Ideas like bones push to break inflated June & like
some carousel, a wave returns the green bucket
here, no wake really just the desert, the very
sop-filled ground where you slip the fold,
blind hills, follow the treeless fields anywhere
else. These are your clothes, arms & legs
& your crumbs. You're child, styrofoam, an atom
boring this planet & circling brightness, look
directly at the sun or drop like man his tiny shovel
nearly for good. To be a hammock, ball struck sharply
from July & tipping your hat, believing a flame
inside the stone & make no mistake what it could be
to be a negative lit. A like, little inkling spit, your head
shaved oh, no more pencils, no teachers, no more
books. With your head an hour to rest, see
when your eyes close no knife, no left hand goddamn
push, push & rerun the round of backyard pools,
sunrise to sunset tag you're it. Some insist we're all
sticks in the spokes & descending, believe it
though we are not. You stand from the summer
& become nearly a husband, nearly a father
who climbs the old, creaking stairs where you hear
so many stories that finish with sleep. When she wakes
you carry your imagined daughter, her name, say

honeybees in clover, plastic slides, slices of a watermelon
& she is not enough to know that you are dead,
that she will never live, not enough that men
stockpile men, bring them under the sky & begin
to slip your chain, ease the room, hood of August now
September & the shrug of October weeds not yet,
no taller in a breeze than dimly for the dirt. In every
fiber blown a new thread needing teethed, to be
that nub of a tooth or the throat in the light no, no
you're seedling, you lift the key in your fingers
to the chorus housing molecule & gleam, thoughts
winged & pure, tungsten, enormous, laughter & shy,
handsome, whorl-like, hopeful, exquisite, luminous, free.

THESE THINGS ASTONISH ME

Feels like rain earshot of the air conditioning
& trees, the first motel doors swung open
toward a breakfast from the continent
I can't identify. Really, the blank lamps
& morning voices, & the shimmer of the pool
you want a little warmer, a little more blue
could be anywhere & my impulse for run-ons
equals my history of lifting one foot, then
another, then get me the hell outta here
& I'm sorry this morning woke as if someone
dropped in a dull quarter, opened my eyes,
started the game over, which is to say
I begin with nothing. Oh one clear phrase
like a light I counted, that yesterday indulged,
let drag & now reels from the furrow back
meaning the sun has up & decided once more
to rise for me & everyone. I've this urge
pitching every breath with the words "my life"
as if I know a thing or two more than this:
my name was right here & in less than a flash
I'll vanish with this courtyard borrowed
for my coffee, my blinking frame who begs
from the world another forever image
lifesaving & new. Please, I ask you please,

& there: treasure of yellow on a wing,
therefore in its breast, the bird blurs past,
cuts the planet I'm still learning clean in half.

IF YOU MEET SOME STRANGER

—for Roshan & Rebecca

Sometimes we stood in rooms & the other fled
as in dreaming. It was home & not our home,
almost you in an airplane folded down stairwells
of a city on the sound. Paper market & moon,
its glint asks, Who braces your tall ladder?
Which side of the coin as it spins across the sole
of a wayward ship? Unbatten, say here I am

looking to hatch. You repeat to the life ring,
see what's next &, yes, let's buy a house
together on the hill & where a wide park scatters
letters, a season each in their making & later
illegible as rain. If elephants land our yard
brand them Little Party Girls, then remember
when you aged, bunked inside a capsule of days,
& the next year you honored the new age.

Let's stop talking here of old hammocks, praise
time when its hold, primitive as ever, passes.
First it is April then May. You welcome
pike rising nearly to song yet turn restless,
it's true, as sometimes we forget those colors
& their fragments flutter away, no advice
whatsoever bestowed. If elephants land the yard,
then hold the periscope & a glass to the wall
for we are better trained in awkwardness:

we say the right thing at the wrong time & call
this distance & groove. You flip on the light
to talk or settle the difference between an inside
& outside joke, startle from the line a crow
who returns with the moon & by no accident
shines on the couple. She's new in town,
I met him at the Laundromat, now we're an item.
We flood the days by the hydrant & wrench

& beneath which chair did we feed the evening
its clothes, telling the truth for good? A true love
is never easy, a good-for-everything turtle
swims & the house in dreaming is small, is gray,
is nestled between an ocean & lake. You spy
something big & blue with white wispy things.
We call it sky. We call it love, & it's magnificent.

Rabbit Beach Road

Relentless as a multiplying thought, miracle
how the lake's rhythm confesses to the air
its riddle, pulsing wild. After the argument

no sunrise cures the day, overcast & below it
(according to the eye) no island. My science
knows better, counters what limping light

lands on the retina's rod, the shifting cones
blind to the indifferent, outstretched hold
unmade by the couch for the husband. Lucky,

my skin doesn't heed the driven mosquitoes
so much as my ear, their buzzing like an arrow
full of yesterday with its stray seeds & stone

constellated over the sand & into the kitchen,
how a crane fly plays so persuasively dead
inside the bed of cauliflower leaves. I pile it

snug in the pocket of a sweatshirt, the hours
I'd picture my father here, join him in ordinary
deference to hummingbird & roadside deer,

hymn for the eagle bald, sublime, dwindling
past the coastal pines. I return to myself dazed
&, while I can, to the shallows where in fact

marbled rocks again outnumber the lake fish
flickering the shore. The waves roll into breath,
six then seven deep after the circle of my iris

dilates & slips, determines the wind & water
entangled, unto itself the boundary ringed
like human needfulness, apology & its mercy,

day after day where the faithful swell renews
no matter, for no better reason than to ask
each body, ours & willingly, to bound right in.

A Recurring Wave of Arrival

Because I believe in devotion to iron, low burner
casting wheat before halved, one each bagged

so we might share a sandwich after saying farewell,
have a good morning & following our separate

lines of shadow not fully fallen, not flat-out
brisk enough to disqualify summer, & because

I am not this or that, him or her or even a match
likely to kindle the delights of a childhood dog,

because in her place I tend to preserve an iodine
blow-by-blow, particulars of the yellow finch

fallen under the glasswork of sky not exactly
caged, nonetheless an interval that often lowers

& sits a minute on our very instinct to breathe,
lays down just so many moments to nap in the dirt

upon the spots of day & because I repeat a dozen,
dozen times an average- to medium-sized word

until it sows a promise, tended then slumped
then buried in cold flowerbeds out along the fence

where the insects have no ego to abandon, hence
go about not like their nouns but in their verbs

present & ablaze, the worker & drones impressing
this tired listener who has more lately leaned,

underwritten another grace in the everyday
when the iron continues to cool & the honeybee

beholds not the drum of raisins on our shelf,
not berries nor cilantro, nor with the compost

shavings of a carrot, not the pestle's leftover dust,
not even flight like fitful sirens on an otherwise

pleasant, nectar-filled afternoon on this planet
sometimes enunciated as mother, & because

my wife found instead this other tiny instinct
asleep in an honest, haphazard urging for grease,

we forget not the preceding week with so much
hinging on another who refused to let us be,

buzzed the din of our kitchen like a loose wire
& across such frequencies we chose to cordon it

half an hour in a clean jar, then a second hour
to prove its act tenacious & alone, to share

with the kids its dimpled crawl, to nearly pull
that very human card by giving it a name & later,

miles away, I looked in time to catch some gold
flickering out a high-rise window & thought,

surely that's our bee, because in olden days
we used to cry out timber & learned to believe

our softer endings sing, leave the spilling red,
oranges & pinks with their ordinary vase to burst

with pregnant flare, tens of thousands of echoes
swelling to bridge the every-which-way paths

sailing like feather from the harbor of our fingers,
off their mooring & eager & yes, if I come back

I'll gather pollen, as many flowers as my nervy
hunger permits in the warmth that sinks the world

or saves it, keeps us coupled, childlike, crazy
for the seasons rubbed together & drawing

our very sparkle toward light, toward my wife
who finds in the grease of our cast iron this eternal

honeybee, broadcasts its surrender to the breeze
where, from what seemed a flowerless place,

I'm humming the first time in months, every bee
bestowing their sweet bounty for the swarm,

for that cloud opening out to color the horizon
& the blossom, oh yes, there's time yet to become.

On the Horse Called Long Shot

—after Ludovico De Luigi

Because there my life was a sure thing, what do I
know now of elegance? The fountain collects
& tilts the coin, the very bronze of muscle
mid-stride, maybe charmed if judgment is chanced
within clouded feelings. But now this is telling,
not showing the world, stay with me
driving the rain, two halves of our city
scribbled with our names. I've worried before
by the wooden bowl sunk under water
too long. In some occasional tree are the cardinals
gone parental, crazy & despite myself I like you
off your clothes & they out the window of a farmhouse
where I warmed years ago. I'm wasting breath.

With your hands you must draw the collective noun
& allow it hunted. This is no memory
when you were a stable & in solid, natural light.
Until I've made a horse I will never be a poet.

I stand too coolly on dying joys, up now
flags for each one. They might be good friends
like you, our fires small in the hayloft over
April nights. Your eyes sparkle wide to touch the filly
& to the festival beneath our ribs, come what may,

put me at ease. Remember, our looks
look great from where I'm looking. Gone,
consider for some the world has yet muttered
its adverb, its comma, its steam. Yes,
our love is spontaneous & never too late.
Yes, this way we trot, by all odds, is exceptional.

The Ballad of Seth & Mona Lisa

Chronology is one way, but I often induce the gaze
crossing ten, twelve years ago when a stranger
locked eyes, coolly, with mine. Possessed,
midstream in a decade & difficult to float us there,
coaxing now the morning at nine, dragging
autumn scenes, limping for a signpost or town,
thirsty water towers, no take backs Georgia,
U-S-of-A. None raise hands beneath the branch
growing tallest or when love breaks ground to say,
You gotta be kidding, you must be teasing & me
often around the twenty-three second mark
dumb, stopped on the tracks, paths we wouldn't
ordinarily & tamping the ill-fated, double-barreled
cannon of thought. Deep in a reddish mound
swarming with ants, only the queen in each family
wears the pants, no idea this her poem & these
my tiny articulations, tiny song parading acorns
everywhere. We measure the maps, we tally
our fingers & cemetery stone before the sky drops
& the Oconee runs, rushes high or all afternoon
hosts the sandbar, lazy swimming holes, fish
believed extinct & clothes in patches of sunlight
to dry. I remember picnics &, in consideration
of his future lending me a pen, my boyishness

flirts with such & such a river twenty years
over, sorting & skipping stone. With little doubt,
come fall, every decent city sways with beauty
& Patrick, most darling barman in all of Athens,
will tell us exactly what we need. We heed
his warning of a left-hand turn, swing the car
steep up the cobblestones for the circle of earth
where the famous oak stands free, owns itself
& the eight-foot spread north & south, east & west
perpetually. I bear these hills no dirty looks,
nor any desire greater than October, backwoods
& their never-ending trees. They stand gold,
held the land before we came to blink & marvel,
taking for a memory one leaf, then two, now three.

LAKE SUPERIOR

Like the breeze, fickle, or how scratching
can crawl, ignore directive, overwhelm
& muscle me from your path, that shapely,

ripe potential at the edge of spring, dreamt
then woke to pitiless, ho-hum highways,
porcupine & deer after a thousandth mile

knocks the calloused, split-tooth towns,
curtains full-length & a limb of leafy shadow
mirrors my fleeting, half-empty life, why

should I seem grievous, blame the summer
our dog folded before the gloss, a final
three then four stairs buckling her story,

fray that only slackens after willing the kids
goodnight, goodbye, one glass of water
adjourned for the bedside hour, its recess

less our bodies if playing mouse, fooling nice
& like lulls of late hummingbirds we twist,
flit, cannot resist so swerve for a sugar

mixing dusk, desire & sometimes the moon
spends an ounce of silver while this lake
heaves, wets, gorges the scrub & my nerve

kisses the glitter as though lamplit & wished,
seeds into grace if we weren't as godless,
off our clothes & (imagine!) I've laid down

driftwood, startled the wings of a monarch
raised now from the dead, honeyed light
aloft & fled with every swell on Rabbit Bay

like breath, raptured, blue coursing blue
where kites, the last ripple of their strings
release, & since the flower that we've sown

must finally nod, let's bless the sun its shade,
embrace, each our living mouths in some
hastened, come-this-way, exhilarated thirst.

Death of the American Hobo

Like any good childhood, I repressed everything,
came up limping, one shoe & caught in a high-rise
lit, hot, twiggy. Corrective: I say I needed
not the arms of heaven but the eternal grapes
of a vineyard, any will do. In college they call me
Carlo Rossi, called me Pissant, me the Gavel
for my muteness seemed as much. Down,
down fell summer & I fished the resulting morning,
stricken at the gutting table. Oh the horrible fish
I've taken, tête-à-tête with some old flame
& I, like a fly, replied in thirty plus directions.
Tempted to say it ducky but I'm brainless
when the cat arrives, robin fetched & what am I
but a wingman messing with that splendor
of a sunrise, self-absorbed, its center beyond hearing
she's getting old & maybe today I'll go home.
I like trains & didn't know best how to tell you
as the fly lands near to better hear the joke
& I killed it, couldn't deny anyone such aloofness
inside the cottontail's eyes, his brown weight
twice the red, red apple across the white
lines of the expressway. Like a hundred chances
fastened, never pursed & just plumb gone.
Should someone else drive or is it that we each

get there in the end? I own no gift but a bell
& where the trout farm closed I've reawakened
under the proverbial tree. I miss the music
flung like seed, tugging away on the lion's ear
before the dog circles knee-deep lightning,
peonies at noon. You look at my garden, shake
all you like your head & these flowers outlive us all.

Every Goddamn Thing an Epilogue

Eyes upward, way up past the cloudy & back
where the whole business of waving accelerates
over fences through goodbyes, interrupting

physically & in various ways a thought becoming
difficult, increasingly backbreaking to pretend
another's shoe traveling in the unseasonably

warm breeze to cherish that which cannot be
unseen: dogs squatting, pinned by the wheel or
surely the old swimming hole buried for good

under weeds. It hasn't been too many years
since we last spoke, forgetting in what question
skulls reconvene, thick with pulse & please

respect the neighbors, their old lawns strewn,
bunches of bunkum, perfect marginalia, inky
shithouse graffiti, politics, doodads, spoilers,

bad jokes. What history I know is everyone
ends up dead, the same sneeze & so we plan,
bend down &, one at a time, we're raising

toasts, rattled by the news that levels our lot
naturally, as when someone great is going,
gone. It's ever the hair of a dog followed home

happily in mind, cordial faces misremembered
& said, altogether shot. I remember sounds
still registering, heads looking out a tilted night,

finding once the rapidly fallen winter. Plus,
we used to smoke in here 'til the neighborhood
sprung, well-lit-oh-well. The last bus swerves

over your place at the curb, it wasn't you
you're elsewhere saying, Look ma, no hands,
wondering what anyone is doing in the left lane

ahead, a decade then two flaring lights, flatbeds
they're really building something & doing so
here. Nights of vinyl & the needles worn,

tables stacked for dancing, jackets who cares
somewhere at the door they said wouldn't ever
be November out with the baby, bathwater

not in December, in life's business stopping
where once insisted some other building & you
swaying these stairs that bridge two rooms

& glad. It's meant to be, never the memory
risen, settling easier as the thing & not its idea
when at times the poets arrive late, stay later

holding court either end of the bar, please
tip generously. A voice brings us to each other
nonetheless looking glum, also on the nose

&, I know, we have to go away. We have to go
back to drinks wearing coasters for a hat,
saying, I worked there once or there my life

so often stood. It happens all in one night
& you shouldn't yet kiss, not cheek nor lips,
not nights assuring you needn't the match

but anyway, maybe I guess you should drive,
don't take it personally. I'm shy with goodbyes
not much more than thank you, even crying

buckets, a highway's worth & their gardens
too a kindness piping its dissonant chord
in & out of town, our ears right on ringing

even asleep & stirring something beautiful,
new, alright. Have a great one, everyone out
& upstanding, loved & the unconditional lifting

hand for a friend until the corners turn, wave
long after she's vanished toward a spot of green
passing it for forest. You can almost smell

wolves among those outlined trees, an inch
leaning this way or that & hope in certain spaces
whole messes lapse, alive, in them our waiting

quick as the glimpse & no doubt we welcome
too much sky, here to stay, our liking not
alone in saying thank you for this everything.

Also by Michael Robins:

The Next Settlement

Ladies & Gentlemen

In Memory of Brilliance & Value

People You May Know is printed in Adobe Garamond Pro.
www.saturnaliabooks.org